JURASSIC POOP

What Dinosaurs (and Others) Left Behind

Written by
Jacob Berkowitz

Illustrated by
Steve Mack

Kids Can Press

In memory of Eric O. Callen, who believed

Text © 2006 Jacob Berkowitz
Illustrations © 2006 Steve Mack

Acknowledgments

This book is one of the first comprehensive surveys of what we know about coprolites and the ancient secrets they reveal. As such, it's possible thanks to the original research of dozens of archaeologists and paleontologists. Special thank yous to: Dr. Glenna Dean, New Mexico State Archaeologist, and Dr. Vaughn M. Bryant, Director, Palynology Laboratory, Department of Anthropology Texas A&M University, for reviewing the text; Dr. Stephen Cumbaa, Research Scientist, Paleobiology, Canadian Museum of Nature, for his endless enthusiasm and tour of the museum's coprolites; Dr. Hendrik Poinar, Assistant Professor, Department of Anthropology, Pathology and Molecular Medicine, McMaster University, for generously sharing his insights and images; and Dr. Karen Chin, for creating and providing seminal paleontological background material. Also thanks to Paul Davidson for his accomplished coprolite camera work. I'm indebted to Robert Callen for sharing the story of his father's life.

I'm grateful to have had Kids Can editor and mentor Valerie Wyatt's wit and wisdom guiding this, my first kids' book. Thanks to KCP's Julia Naimska for inspired design, Lisa Tedesco for tracking down photos and Steve Mack for telling the Jurassic Poop story in images.

Kids Can Press gratefully acknowledges the financial support of the Government of Ontario, through the Ontario Media Development Corporation; the Ontario Arts Council; the Canada Council for the Arts; and the Government of Canada, through the CBF, for our publishing activity.

Published in Canada and the U.S. by Kids Can Press Ltd.
25 Dockside Drive, Toronto, ON M5A 0B5

Kids Can Press is a Corus Entertainment Inc. company

www.kidscanpress.com

Edited by Valerie Wyatt
Designed by Julia Naimska

Printed and bound in Buji, Shenzhen, China, in 12/2018 by WKT Company

CM 06 0 9 8 7 6 5 4 3
CM PA 06 0 9 8

Library and Archives Canada Cataloguing in Publication

Berkowitz, Jacob
    Jurassic poop : what dinosaurs (and others) left behind / written by Jacob Berkowitz ; illustrated by Steve Mack.

ISBN 978-1-55337-860-0 (bound)
ISBN 978-1-55337-867-9 (pbk.)

1. Coprolites—Juvenile literature. 2. Fossils—Food—Juvenile literature. I. Mack, Steve (Steve Page) II. Title.

QE899.2.C67B47 2006   j567.9   C2005-904318-0

CONTENTS

CHAPTER 1
A MESSAGE FROM A BOTTOM

Under a warm sun, one of the biggest predators of all time paces across a river delta. A tyrannosaurid's massive feet slosh through the shallow, stagnant water. Then the six-story-tall killer, a relative of *Tyrannosaurus rex,* briefly pauses. He feels an urge and slightly raises his massive tail. A tyrannosaurid turd larger than two loaves of bread plunges into the water.

Some minnows zip over to examine the dropping. Bits of shattered and partly digested bone from a pachycephalosaur (a duck-billed dinosaur) poke out of the king-sized poop.

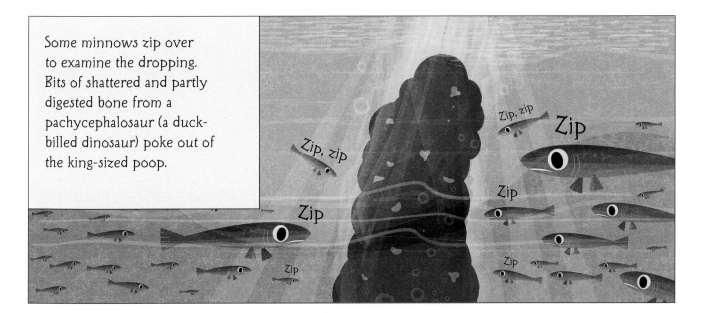

That night heavy rain falls in the nearby highlands. Water carrying sand and silt rushes into the river, and the water level at the delta slowly rises. The tyrannosaurid turd, now long forgotten by its maker, disappears under a layer of sand and mud — forever.

Or so you might think. But 75 million years later, near Onefour, Alberta, a sharp-eyed dinosaur hunter makes one whopper of a paleo-poop-and-scoop. And if you think this is just a tall tale, turn the page, because she's got the poop to prove it!

Wow!

King of the Coprolites*

Only two tyrannosaurid coprolites have ever been found, and this one from Onefour, Alberta, is the biggest.

Scientists think the pooper was either a Daspletosaurus or a Gorgosaurus, earlier relatives of T. rex. These were the only carnivores in the area at the time large enough to produce this massive mound.

The white covering is a plaster cast that the poop was wrapped in to hold it together and protect it.

This measurement scale tells you the coprolite's size, about 64 cm (2 ft.) long and 17 cm (6 1/2 in.) wide.

*Coprolites

The polite word for fossil feces is coprolite, which comes from the Greek words *kopros* for "dung" and *lithus* for "rock." So a coprolite is a turd that's turned to rock, although not all coprolites are as preserved as rock.

Coprolites are trace fossils. This means they're not an actual preserved part of an animal or plant, like a bone or tooth, but rather something that a creature left behind. Footprints, skin impressions and eggs are also trace fossils. Scientists use trace fossils, including coprolites, to help piece together the puzzle of ancient life.

Along with bits of bone, this coprolite contains undigested dinosaur meat, indicating that tyrannosaurids gulped their food.

5 cm

Fossil Poo? No Way!

Fossil poo? No way, you might say. How could something that soft and gooey survive a week, let alone millions of years? Well, hang on to your seat, because fossil feces are everywhere.

Just think about how much stooping and pooping has gone on since the beginning of life on Earth. You could call our planet a poop factory. Plants convert sunlight into food, animals digest

Coprofact

During a lifetime you'll dump far more than your body weight in dung.

Coprofact

The soil we grow our food in is largely made from the poo of worms and other small animals.

to learn the secrets these gems hold. And, you guessed it, archaeologists have even found lots of ancient human heaps.

Given the amount of dung that's been deposited, it only makes sense that some of this stinky stuff has survived the long journey from fresh to fossil.

Really old doo-doo has been found on every continent and from hundreds of kinds of ancient animals. Dino dung, ancient shark poop, mammoth mounds — they've all been scooped up by scientists eager

the plants into feces, then insects and bacteria eat the poop and release nutrients that feed plants. It's the great cycle of life, and poop helps hold it all together.

Fecal or Fiction?

There's no tell-tale stink. It's no longer squishy. So how do you know when you've found a real coprolite? The problem is, a rock can be a dead ringer for ancient dung. Or an ordinary-looking rock can actually be a piece of paleo-poop.

To sort the real poop from the pretenders, scientists use a coprolite checklist.

☑ Location

Where did you find the specimen? Was it in a fossil deposit along with fossil bones or teeth? If so, then you have evidence that there were animals around who could have been the poopers.

☑ Shape

Having a poopy shape is often the first sign that a rock is a coprolite. But not always. A specimen might just be a piece of a larger coprolite and so not look at all like dung.

Found frozen — the shape helps tell us it's arctic fox poop.

☑ Contents

Does your specimen contain the remains of the last meal? Are there bones, fish scales or pieces of plants? If yes, you're one step closer to determining that it's a coprolite.

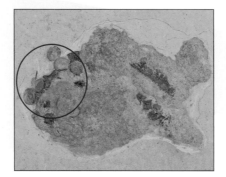

The fish bones (circled) in this specimen are a good clue it's a coprolite.

☑ Chemistry

A coprolite has a different chemical composition than surrounding rocks. For example, a carnivore's coprolite should contain more phosphate (from the calcium phosphate in the bones of its prey) than nearby rock.

Fly-sized fish coprolites from an ancient ocean that once covered the Canadian prairies

☑ Burrows

Has something been eating that excrement? Yuck! But evidence of dung beetle burrows makes it an almost open-and-shut case that you've got a coprolite. Look for signs of burrowing — tiny holes or circles of different-colored rock on the surface, which are evidence of in-filled holes.

An ancient crocodile coprolite with insect burrows

The Salmon Creek Mystery

Could the world's most famous fossil feces be fake?

One look at the rocks along the banks of Salmon Creek in Washington State and you want to hold your nose. They have a ropy shape and pinched ends, just like fresh doggy doo-doo in your local park. And they have lines along the side that appear to be rectal striations, marks caused when the poop made its final exit. They're even sold in museums as coprolites.

But hold on a minute, say scientists who have taken a closer look. Something doesn't smell quite right.

When these curlicues are cut up, there's no evidence of plant or animal remains in them. And they usually aren't found alongside other fossils. So there's no evidence of predators, prey or plants.

What gives the rocks their poopy shape? One explanation is that there was lots of gas, but no poop. The specimens are found in rocks that were formed above those with lots of plant remains.

Is it a coprolite or is it a fake? This Salmon Creek specimen sure looks like the real thing.

When the plants decayed they produced methane. That's a gas that's also in, well, farts. Over time the methane gas built up in pockets, just like in your bowel, until the earth "farted." As this gas traveled through a muddy layer, it pushed liquid mud through cracks in the rock above. When the pressure was released, the cracks pinched shut. (Sounds kind of familiar, doesn't it?) The result? What might be the world's best coprolite copycats.

muddy layer

pockets of methane

plant remains

Poop Imposters!

When looking for coprolites, don't be fooled — there are lots of look-alikes. Even experienced coprolite collectors can be confused by these poop imposters.

Concretions, conglomerates and coprolites — they may look alike, but only one started at an animal's rear end.

Concretions are chunks of clay or limestone that form around a hard object, such as a rock or shell. They are often eroded by wind and water into interesting poop-like shapes.

Conglomerates are rocks made up of lots of smaller rocks or bits of shell and fossils that are held together by a natural mineral cement. All these add-

It looks like a fossilized cow patty, but it's a concretion.

ons can make conglomerates look suspiciously like coprolites.

Vomit or poop? Sometimes paleontologists have a hard time figuring out which end the remains of an ancient meal came out of. Like many present-day animals, some ancient animals regurgitated (vomited up) bits of bone and fur that were too big to take the regular escape route.

To identify ancient vomit, look for big bones that don't have any stomach acid etching on the surface from being digested.

Beware! If you think you've got a coprolite, be sure it's not a cololite. That's food that was eaten by an ancient animal, but was fossilized in its intestines when the animal died. *Oh, just a little longer and I would have been a coprolite!*

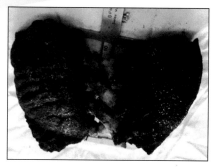

Cololites in the colon of a mummified body

A COPROLITE WITH A SHELL?

Sometimes it's the poop that's the imposter. Scientists

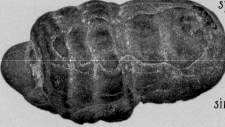

collecting fossils in Antarctica found this spiral-shaped specimen. Must be a snail, they thought, and put it on the museum shelf.

Years later, another group of scientists found lots of similar fossils nearby. But they

realized there was something fishy about them. Many kinds of fish, including sharks, have spiral-shaped intestines and squeeze-out spiral poops. And that snail? You guessed it — it was really fish feces.

Reverend William Buckland

He's famous as one of the first paleontologists to identify dinosaur bones. But the Reverend William Buckland was also the world's first paleo-poop scooper.

In the 1820s, Reverend Buckland went searching for fossils along the ocean beach at Lyme Regis in southern England. He filled his blue cloth bag with the fossil bones of ancient marine reptiles, such as ichthyosaurs, and the beautiful spiral fossil shells of giant squid-like nautoloids.

But some of the fossils he found were real head scratchers. They were odd fossils that he said looked like an "oblong pebble or kidney potatoes." And, if cut lengthways, these fossils had a distinctive spiral shape.

Another fossil collector thought they were ancient pinecones. No way, said Reverend Buckland.

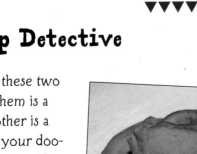

When he saw bits of bone in his spiral specimens he knew he'd bagged some really ancient doo-doo and gave them the name "coprolites."

You Be the Poop Detective

Take a close look at these two specimens. One of them is a real coprolite. The other is a poop imposter. Use your doo-doo detective skills to see if you can tell the coprolite from the fake. Answer on page 39.

CHAPTER 2
FROZEN, DRIED OR LITHIFIED

From the moment it hits the ground, a coprolite-in-training learns that the world is a dangerous place.

One big rain and you're mush.

And it *seems* everyone wants to eat you.

One careless step and you're a footprint.

Are you going to win the lottery of leftovers and make the passage from feces to fossil? Or will you take the fecal fast track and decay? If you want to last, your only hope is to be frozen, dried or lithified.

Survival of the Feces

So which dropping will make it to posterity? It's a question of the survival of the feces.

The science of how things fossilize is called taphonomy. To study taphonomy, scientists watch how things decay. The slower doo-doo decays, the better its chance of becoming a coprolite.

Some dedicated field researchers have determined that, in the United Kingdom, the average cow patty sweats it out for 114 days in summer before breaking down. In winter, it can make it to the ripe old age of 173 days. That's kids' stuff for North American mounds. In California, cow patties can make it to 500 days, and in the Canadian cold, cow pies can tough it out for years.

These differences in rates of decay are due to temperature, amounts of rain and snow and the creatures that all coprolites fear — insects.

Insects love to chow down on fresh feces. Dung beetles and flies are the top doo-doo diners. The situation is much worse for turds from herbivores (plant eaters) than for those from carnivores (meat eaters). Carnivores digest most of their meal, leaving little nutrition in their nuggets to attract insects. But herbivores gnaw on tough grasses, leaves and bark, and much of the food value remains in the feces. So if you're a dropping from a mammoth or a triceratops — both herbivores — you're going to have to be a lot luckier to make it from fresh to fossil.

Scats on Ice

If you live where it snows in winter, you've probably seen lots of frozen dog doo-doo. But most frozen feces are one-season wonders. They turn to mush in the warm spring sunshine. Under just the right conditions, though, poop that gets a chilly reception can hang around for thousands of years.

Frozen ancient reindeer droppings have been found in northern Russia. (*Rudolph?*) And the remains of a last meal have been found in Ice Age mammoths and horses preserved in permafrost in Alaska and northern Canada. The most amazing coprolite coolers are ice patches in northern mountains. These piles of snow and ice, often nestled into a nook on the north side of a mountain, can survive not just one summer but thousands of them — and so

can any feces trapped in them. This makes ice patches great turd time capsules.

In 1997, a hiker was enjoying the fresh air in the mountains near Whitehorse, Yukon Territory, when she raised her nose and did a double sniff. Whoa! The fresh alpine air suddenly smelled like a barnyard. Her nose had led her to the world's most fantastic frozen feces. And some of them were melting and raising a stink. She'd found an ice patch full of layers of caribou poo.

Scientists have now discovered about seventy of these ice patches in Yukon Territory, and they're all full of it. Eight thousand years of the stuff! And similar poopy ice patches have also been found in Alaska. So how did the caribou pellets hit the deep freeze?

In the summer, caribou hate the heat and biting bugs. Off they

go up a mountain to their naturally air-conditioned, bug-free ice patch. Which is what hundreds of generations of caribou did and still do. The result is ice patches that look like cakes, with alternating layers of chocolate (poop) and vanilla (snow and ice).

Some of the patches are huge — as long as ten soccer fields end to end and as deep as a nine-story building is high. In some patches, layers of poop and snow have melted into a super layer — a century of condensed caribou poop in a single sludgy sheet. But in other places, thousand-year-old pellets look as fresh as the day they first hit the snow.

Melting ice patches reveal frozen black caribou coprolites.

Don't Forget
The Bag and Chain Saw

How do you collect feces in ice? You hire a glaciologist who straps on his crampons, grabs his chain saw and cuts out blocks of ice all the way up the face of the ice patch. The blocks are kept in plastic bags in a walk-in freezer so that scientists can study them.

One day these frozen samples could be all that remains of the poopy ice patches. The northern climate is warming, and the ice patches are rapidly melting. If this continues, soon only a dried-out decomposing dung field will remain as the end of an amazing tale.

Dried Doo-Doo

For poop that can't chill out, the next best thing is to dry out. Think about what happens to a grape that's left out in a nice dry spot. The water slowly evaporates, and the grape shrivels up and becomes a raisin. Gentle, slow drying can also turn poop into a coprolite. After several thousand years, once-soft, wet poop becomes as brittle and hard as rock. Deserts and high-altitude places, such as the Andes Mountains in Peru and Chile, are great spots for finding dried coprolites that have survived since the last ice age.

I'm drying!

Coprolites in Caves

If you're looking for dried coprolites, check out caves and rock overhangs. These sheltered areas protect poop from wind and rain. And because they're sheltered, they attract many different kinds of poopers.

The first coprolites ever discovered were dried Ice Age hyena droppings found in a British cave in 1823.

In Wales, the Ogof Draenen cave system has a hip-deep heap of fossilized bat guano. Ancient bats made this mess when Roman emperor Julius Caesar was calling the shots.

Mylodon Cave in southern Chile is an Ice Age poop park. For more than 60 000 years, Ice Age animals, including mammoths and ground sloths, relieved themselves in this cave, which is big enough to hold a 747 jet. Those poopers left a whopping 9 m (30 ft.) thick pile of dried doo-doo. That's not a mound, that's a mountain!

An Ice Age ground sloth coprolite found in Mylodon Cave, Chile

Wendy Sloboda

Want to find coprolites? Take some pointers from Alberta's Wendy Sloboda. As a teenager, Wendy found Canada's first dino eggs and the world's first dino footprints with skin impressions. But that was just a warm-up. Since then she's found the world's only two tyrannosaurid turds, one in Saskatchewan and the other in Alberta. Her friends are so impressed they call her the Turdanator! Now she works as a fossil finder and fixer with the world's top dino hunters, traveling to Mongolia, Argentina and France in search of fantastic fossils.

So how do you spot fossil feces? Wendy says watch where you step. She's seen people walk right over fossils and miss them. Here are her top three turd-spotting tips:

1 Head for the desert. Most fossil hunting takes place in dry, desert-like areas with lots of sun.

2 Walk fast and long. The more ground you cover, the better your chance of getting lucky.

3 Watch how the sun reflects off the ground. Look for objects that stand out because of their shape, color or texture.

Lithify Me!

So you want to be lithified (turned into stone)? To make the perilous passage from rump to rock, follow these instructions carefully. It might take tens of thousands of years, but once you're rock solid you'll last for millions more.

Step #1: A solid start

If you want a chance to end up rock hard, it helps to have a firm start. That's why it's best if you're a carnivore dropping that's already packed with hard materials, such as undigested bone, shell or fur. But don't despair if you're the end of a herbivore's meal. Even herbivore pellets can be pretty solid, especially if they have time to dry.

Hurray!

Step #2: Pray for a soft landing and take cover

Shout *Hurray!* if your final resting place is on soft sand, silt or mud. All you need now is a covering of more sand, silt or mud, either in the water or blown by the wind. It might feel a little scary at first (*Gee, it's dark in here*). But slowly, year upon year, layer upon layer, you'll be safely buried in sediment.

Over millions of years, pressure from the sediment on top will make the layers around you solidify into rocks such as limestone, sandstone and mudstone. And you'll turn into rock along with them.

Step #3: Stay still

Getting (*ahem!*) deposited was enough movement. Don't go getting pushed around or you'll get all broken up. If you're on land, hope there isn't a torrential rainfall. If you're in the water, stay away from currents and waves that could send you tumbling. The best place to be is a still lagoon or swamp or in deep water where it's calm.

Help!

Step #4: Wait for help

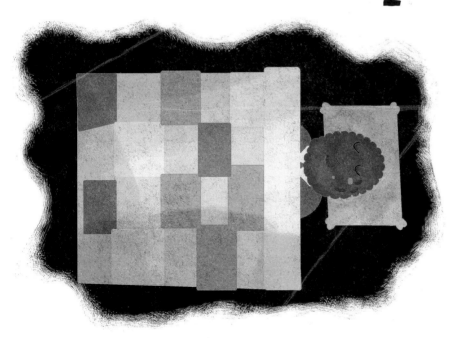

Don't panic! You're so close to wearing the coprolite crown. Just let the minerals come to you. Inside your turdy tomb, you're going to be permineralized — minerals from the surrounding sediment will begin seeping into you. Say goodbye to organic matter, such as partly digested grass or meat, as it's gently filled or replaced by these minerals. Even your bacteria are lending a hand. They create a chemical environment that helps minerals move in.

This lithified coprolite from Saskatchewan, Canada, is a handful.

You've made it! You've gone through a mineral movement, and now you're the same color and smell as the surrounding rock. For example, coprolites in mudrocks (rocks formed from mud) smell muddy. And scientists think that's a lot better than your original smell.

Coprolite Crafts

You know how the real ones are made and what they look like. Now it's time to make your own coprolite with copro-dough you can make yourself.

You'll need:
- 500 mL (2 cups) all-purpose flour
- 125 mL (1/2 cup) salt
- about 250 mL (1 cup) warm water
- optional: food coloring or tempera paint

1 Mix the flour and salt together and add enough of the water to make the dough into a ball. (Start with 175 mL [3/4 cup] of water and add more as needed.)

2 Knead the ball of dough for about 5 minutes, until it feels soft and easy to squeeze.

3 Shape the ball (or parts of it) into one or more coprolites. Let your coprolite air-dry for several days.

Hints: For best drying results, make your coprolites less than 2.5 cm (1 in.) thick. Store unused copro-dough in a bag in the refrigerator so it doesn't dry out.

Turd to Treasure

Wow, that's a beautiful coprolite you're wearing. Jurassic poop jewelry? Yep! A dropping's journey to jewelry starts when it's turned into an agate. These gemstones form when rocks and fossils (including coprolites) are covered by volcanic ash and water. Depending on the mix of minerals, agates can have beautiful streaks and swirls of red, white, yellow or blue.

Jewelry-makers cut, tumble and polish pieces of agate into beautiful shiny, rounded gems. Coprolite agates are used to make everything from earrings to belt buckles and even rings. Now that's a special way to say I love you!

An agatized coprolite cut and polished to a gleam

REALLY WELL-AGED MANURE

The world's most famous coprolites are the ones that launched a revolution in the way we grow our food.

In the 1840s, farmers in England didn't have enough animal manure to fertilize their crops. The solution? Dinosaur coprolites. Hundreds of people in southeastern England were hired to dig up coprolites, which are rich in calcium phosphate, a main ingredient in fertilizer. Ground up and mixed with sulfuric acid, the coprolites became the world's first artificial fertilizer.

As it turned out, only some of these "coprolites" were the real thing — most of the stuff dug up was just rock. But that didn't stop the people of Ipswich from naming a street Coprolite Street. The townsfolk of Bassingbourn went even further — to commemorate their coprolite history they erected a statue of a pile of dino poo.

CHAPTER 3

WHO DUNG IT?

You're walking along enjoying the view when suddenly you step in it. Or rather on it. It's a rock-hard coprolite from some ancient animal. But which animal?

For scientists this is the million-dollar question. You might have the best specimen in the world, but if you don't know who dung it, your coprolite can't tell you much about the long-ago past.

To determine the poopetrator, you'll have to use a process of elimination. That's how scientists do it. The goal is to eliminate as many potential poopers as possible and narrow the list of contenders by asking some hard questions.

When Was It Pooped?

The answer to this question will help narrow the list of potential poopers.

How do you determine a fossil's age? Your specimen has two "ages": its relative age and its absolute age.

A fossil's relative age is how old it is in comparison with other fossils and rocks around it. (Think of it this way: if you have a younger sister and an older brother, your relative age is in the middle.)

To figure out relative age, scientists identify the various layers of sedimentary rock where the coprolite was found and their position in relation to one another. The top layer is always younger than the layer underneath it.

By knowing the relative age of the rock where your coprolite was found, you can eliminate a lot of poopetrators. For example, if the rock layer is relatively recent, you can scratch the dinosaurs off the list.

Absolute age is a fossil's exact age in calendar years. (It's like saying: I'm ten and a half years old.) For a specimen younger than 50 000 years old, scientists use a technique called carbon dating to determine absolute age. When they breathe, all animals take in tiny amounts of carbon 14, a type of radioactive carbon. Some of it ends up in their poop. By studying how much carbon is left in a coprolite, scientists can figure out how old it is to within a few decades.

Where Was It Found?

OK, you've got the date of the dump, now let's move on to check out the surroundings. Was it pooped in water or on land? That will tell you a lot about the pooper. Check the surrounding rocks and other nearby fossils. If you found your coprolite close to lots of fish fossils, the poop probably came from them or other aquatic animals. And by examining those fish fossils, you'll be able to tell whether your coprolite was pooped in fresh water or in a salty sea.

If you found your coprolite in a cave, do some sleuthing at the scene. Are there animal bones nearby that could provide clues as to the poopetrator? Are there any human tools, such as stone arrows or blades? Maybe your specimen came from someone who looked remarkably like you.

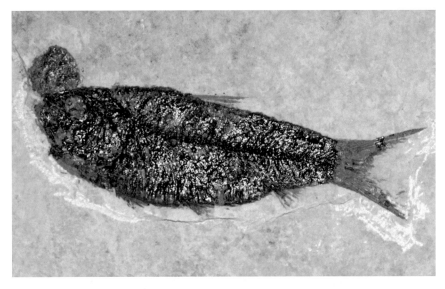

This coprolite (the blob above the fish's head) was probably made by a fish.

What Does It Look Like?

The more clearly you can describe your coprolite's size, shape and texture, the more easily you can compare it with coprolites that have already been identified. Maybe you'll find a match.

Start with size. Measure that mound, but don't jump to conclusions. Tiny turds can come from big animals. After all, the mighty moose sometimes poops pellets the size of peanuts. But if you've got a whopper, you can scratch smaller animals off your list.

To help you ID your fossil turd, you'll need the right words to describe it. No, "gross" and "wow" won't do. Scientists have to be more precise. They ask:
- What color is it, inside and out?
- Is it cylindrical, conical or spherical?
- Does it have constrictions (areas where it gets thinner and then wider)?
- Is its texture homogeneous (all the same) or aggregate (a mixture of parts)?
- Is it entire or in pieces?
- Is it friable (crumbly) or really hard?

Now you can paint a perfect word picture of your poop.

What's Inside It?

To make the link between droppings and dropper, you often need to get inside your fossil feces. Sometimes you can pry the stuff apart. But really hard doo-doo is often studied by slicing off paper-thin, see-through sections, which are examined under a microscope.

Whatever the method, the contents of a mound can tell you if your poopetrator was a herbivore or a carnivore. If you see bones, bingo! It was a carnivore. Microscopic pollen and plant fibers tell you the pooper was a herbivore.

Tiny parasites, or their eggs, in poop are a great find. Most parasites are very picky about where they call home. Usually they inhabit only one type of animal. The roundworm *Trichuris trichiura,* for example, only lives in humans. Finding one of these parasites in a turd makes it an open-and-shut case. Your coprolite is ancient human doo-doo.

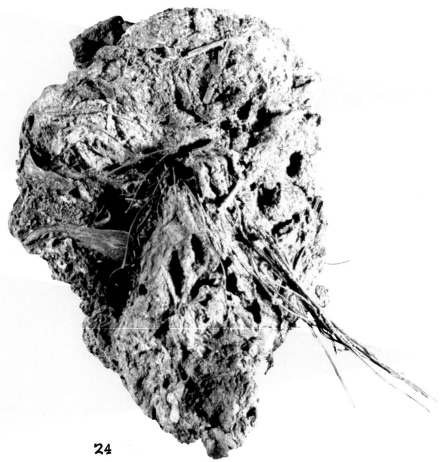

An ancient Native American coprolite from Texas. Notice all the plant material.

How Does It Compare to the Fresh Stuff?

Scientists study scat (feces) from living animals to find out more about them. This is called the science of scatology. Scatologists have detailed field guides for identifying wild scat. By comparing your ancient specimen with modern scat, you just might find a family resemblance that will help identify the pooper. For example, paleontologists think that many smooth coprolites they find are from alligators. Today's alligators completely digest the bones in their meal, making smooth, pasty poops, and their ancient relatives probably did too.

Solve the Case of Who Dung It!

Are you ready to solve a coprolite mystery? Take a close look at this coprolite and the three potential poopetrators. Use the clues to help match the maker with its mound. Answer on page 39.

Clues
- Age:
  about 75 million years old
- Where found:
  Northeast Texas, U.S.A.
  (Hint: 70 million years ago this area was covered by a large sea.)
- Contents:
  pieces of broken and crushed bone
- Size:
  5 cm (2 in.) long

Potential poopetrators
- Ancient shark (these animals make distinctive spiral poops) Ⓐ
- Mosasaur (a carnivorous marine reptile) Ⓑ
- Velociraptor (a land-loving hunter) Ⓒ

The Great Name Debate

Once you've ID'd your coprolite, should you give it a name? (*Oh, he's so cute, let's call him Sludge!*) It's not as crazy as it sounds. Each species of animal and plant on Earth has a special two-part Latin name that scientists around the world use to avoid confusion. Humans are *Homo* (man) *sapiens* (wise). Or there's *Tyrannosaurus rex*.

But a species name for fossil feces? Hey, other trace fossils, like eggs and footprints, get Latin names. There's *Skartopus australis,* a 75-million-year-old footprint of a dinosaur found in Australia. Why not coprolites?

Well, say some scientists, it's not because they come from the wrong side of the digestive track. It's just that there's not much consistency among coprolites. Bones and teeth have a similar shape from one individual to the next. One triceratops femur (thigh bone) looks pretty much like the next. Even their footprints will be similar. But the shape, size and contents of their feces change from dump to dump.

So call your coprolite what you want, say many paleontologists, but don't call it *Turdus maximus.*

Don't Scoop That Poop!

Most of the time people are happy if you pick up poop, but not if that poop is a coprolite. As with other fossils, paleontologists sigh when they see coprolites collected and sold to the highest bidder. Yes, you can buy dinosaur dung and other coprolites from fossil dealers. Often they're sold as joke items. So what's the problem?

Unfortunately, most coprolites are sold without information on exactly where they're from. Once this location information is lost, the fossil can't tell us much.

There are laws in various countries, states and provinces to try and save coprolites and other fossils for all to enjoy and learn from. So check before you collect.

Karen Chin

Who do you call if you want the dirt on dinosaur coprolites? Karen Chin's the name, dinosaur dung's the game.

Karen is a paleoecologist (a scientist who studies the relationships between ancient animals, plants and the environment). And she's the only one in the world whose full-time window on the past is fossil doo-doo. Her office at the University of Colorado is full of it. She's had her hands on thousands of fossilized turds, from giant tyrannosaurid coprolites to ancient marine reptile coprolites from the high Arctic.

As a young girl, Karen never dreamed what she'd

end up studying. She began learning about fossil plants and bones. As she looked at plant remains in fossil feces, she soon realized there was a more fertile field of research. It's the coprolites, she realized, that hold the clues to how and what dinosaurs and other

ancient animals ate and the role their poop played in the great cycle of life.

Her hunch about the value of coprolites has paid off. She's found the earliest case of dung beetles eating poop — they dined on dino droppings 75 million years ago. And she's even found evidence that some dinosaurs snacked on rotten wood.

Her goal is to create a coprolite family tree that will help scientists link poops and poopetrators. With this, she'll have turned ancient turds into powerful scientific tools. Because when you know who dung it, there's a great story you can tell.

CHAPTER 4

TOILET TALES

How will you make your mark in history? Sometimes it's not about being number one, but rather doing a number two. Yep, we're talking about human coprolites.

Most of us do our business, give it a flush and wash our hands of the whole thing. But before the invention of the toilet, turds weren't flushed — they were dropped at the back of caves or into pit outhouses or privies. Some of these leavings have become amazing postcards from the past. And, boy, are archaeologists happy to find them. Coprolites have the poop on ancient people like nothing else, from what and how they ate, to their diseases and even their pets!

AIRMAIL

Max and Francesca
2 Privy Lane
Merry Old England

Hi!
Had a long trip down, but the landing was soft. Seems I only bought a one-way ticket.
Wish you were here.
Your friend,

Poo

Poop Patrol

Where do you find ancient human poop? Almost anywhere people have lived. The oldest human coprolites found so far are 300 000-year-old coprolites discovered along the southern coast of France, at Terra Amata. For more recent specimens, the privies of castles, forts and simple homes are great places to find old poop. And since these buildings were often used for hundreds of years, there's been lots of time for specimens to build up.

This 50 000-year-old Neanderthal coprolite was found in Gibraltar Cave, Spain.

Texan Turd Treasure

Just how many human coprolites can you find in one place? The load doesn't get any bigger than at Hinds Cave in the Chihuahuan desert in southwest Texas.

Hinds Cave is cut high into a cliff overlooking the desert. So it has a superb view. Obviously, ancient people agreed — Hinds Cave was the place to stop and go for generations. More than a thousand perfectly preserved dried turds have been collected from a prehistoric poop pile at the back of the cave. The turds found here were deposited by people over the course of about 8000 years.

Most of the turds are about 95 percent fiber — that's about fifteen times the amount of fiber you eat daily, and it's why some of the coprolites look like cow patties. The fiber comes from local desert plants, including prickly pear cactus, agave and yucca. But like today's Texans, these ancient people also liked their meat. The coprolites contain the bones from sixteen different kinds of animals, including packrats, antelope, birds and fish. Which gives Hinds Cave another claim to fame — site of the first Texan surf and turf.

Your turn ...

History from the Bottom Up

E ureka! That's the sound of an archaeologist finding an outhouse. Not because she has to go, but because she wants to dig.

What makes outhouses (a.k.a. privies, latrines, loos) such exciting finds? It's because they're amazing preservers. Look down into the hole of an outhouse and you'll see why. All that sloppy poop and pee piles up, leaving no room for bacteria to breathe. Yes, there's almost no oxygen down there in the poop pile. This means that the bacteria that decompose the dung do it anaerobically (without oxygen). This type of decomposition is very slow, and materials such as leather, bones and seeds barely decay at all.

Digging down is like peeling back the pages of time — the top is the most recent and the bottom is the deep, dark past. But leave the privy digging to the pros. Dangerous viruses and bacteria can survive in privies for hundreds and sometimes thousands of years.

There's no oxygen in here!

We're suffocating!

Privy Gold

Long-ago privies collected a lot more than poop. They were handy places to dump household wastes, everything from broken plates to food scraps and even old clothes. And they were also good places to hide things, like booze bottles and even bodies. For example, at Fort Wellington, Canada, 150 years ago, pets weren't allowed. But we know the soldiers broke the rules: the remains of puppies are in the privy. Whoever put the bodies there thought it was a sure thing nobody would ever find them — at least not for a couple of hundred years.

Ancient Menus Revealed

Want to know what people were eating in days of old? The ancient kitchen might be bare, but you can bet the outhouse has a story to tell.

❶ Medieval cesspits, Kiel, Germany

The people of Kiel liked their veggies.

The town's cesspits contain thirty-nine types of wild and cultivated plants as well as exotic overseas spices, including pepper. There are also the remains of hops, meaning folks were washing down their meals with beer.

❷ Latrine drains, Paisley Abbey, Scotland, 15th century

What was on a medieval monk's menu? This latrine contains bones that show that the monks chowed down on beef, pork, lamb, goat and also fish and shellfish.

❸ Latrine, 1st-century Roman soldiers' quarters, near Amsterdam, Holland

The Roman Empire made sure their centurions (soldiers) had tasty meals. Latrine remains indicate their food was garnished with fennel, caraway, aniseed, dill and coriander. Someone was even sending care packages — the latrine contains peach pits, a luxury item not grown in Europe at the time.

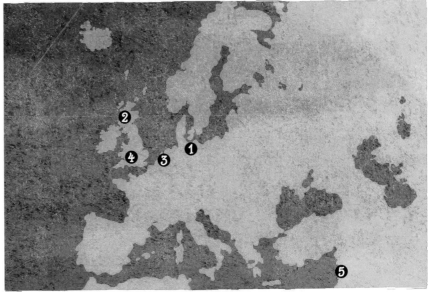

❹ Latrine, Dudley Castle, England, 1642–47

The soldiers stationed here during the English civil war ate lots of fruit. Their latrine contains loads of seeds and pits from strawberries, figs, grapes, cherries, plums, apples and pears.

❺ Cesspit, 700 B.C., City of David, Jerusalem

People here liked their meat rare — very rare. Their cesspit contains lots of parasite eggs, indicating that the meat they ate was undercooked.

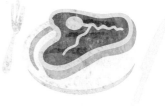

Squatting for Science

Studying pollen in coprolites is a great way to see what ancient people were eating. Pollen has a tough coating that often keeps it from being digested. So it's a long-term survivor, even in poop. Just one hitch: was the pollen found in a coprolite from the person's last meal or from a feast a month earlier?

Archaeologist Glenna Dean decided to find out just how long it takes different kinds of pollen to pass through the human digestive system. She had volunteers, including herself, record what they ate each day. Then she collected the, um,

Been here long?

Nope. You?

leftovers and froze them. Later, under a laboratory fume hood (*crank up the suction!*), she thawed her specimens and identified and counted the pollen.

It turns out that there are big differences in how quickly pollen makes it to the end zone. The bigger and heavier the pollen grain, the faster it travels. But small pollen grains, like those of broccoli, can hang around your bowels for months. So the pollen in a single poop could span a month of meals.

Unpooped Poop

The rarest, but most exciting place to find old poop is inside the pooper. Cololites (unpooped poops) are found in mummified bodies around the world. Some of these bodies naturally dried out in desert caves. Others were frozen into glaciers or preserved in bogs (acidic wetlands). And then there are the famous Egyptian mummies.

Cololites in a mummified human body can give scientists a snapshot of exactly what that ancient person was eating. One of the most famous bog people is Grauballe Man in Denmark. He was killed in a human sacrifice and buried in a bog about 2000 years ago. His cololites and stomach contents show that his last meal was a gruel that included barley, oats and willow herb. There's no fruit, so he was probably buried in winter.

Teams of scientists have studied the cololites from an amazing 5300-year-old Iceman. His frozen corpse was found in 1991 on a glacier high in the Alps. Examination of his cololites showed that he had recently eaten bread made from hand-ground wheat and also meat, possibly that of an ibex (mountain goat).

Eric O. Callen

In the 1950s and 1960s, most archaeologists only laughed about the human coprolites they found and threw them away. Not McGill University professor Eric Callen. He believed these ancient human feces held valuable scientific secrets. During World War II, he'd been a British spy working to help crack secret German codes. Now he set about to be a coprolite cracker.

His first mission: figure out how to remove the contents of a coprolite without damaging them. The problem? The Peruvian poops he first studied were rock solid, and it was

impossible to pull out their contents without destroying the specimen. Mr. Callen's solution was to throw them back in the toilet — actually a beaker full of trisodium phosphate. The coprolites

soaked up the liquid and, after forty-eight hours, were back to their old soft selves — including the smell!

When Mr. Callen examined the contents of seeds and bits of plants in the coprolites, he realized he was right. Here were amazing secrets about the first foods ancient people grew, such as maize, and even clues to how they prepared their meals.

The Callen technique of soaking coprolites is still in use today. Sadly, Eric Callen himself died in 1970 in the mountains of Peru, while doing what he loved best — studying ancient Inca coprolites.

Are You an Outhouse Detective?

Look at these specimens collected from an old outhouse. Can you identify the foods the outhouse users were eating? (And what can you tell about the age of at least one of the outhouse users?) Answers on page 39.

CHAPTER 5
LESSONS FROM LEAVINGS

You can learn a lot from an old turd. That coprolite is full of fascinating stories about ancient times. If you listen closely, a coprolite will tell you about the animal it came from, the creature's health, eating behavior (did it chew or gulp?) and what or whom it ate. The coprolite may even reveal information about the surrounding environment, such as the kinds of plants that grew there. Which is why more and more scientists are taking lessons from ancient leavings.

Lesson #1: Coprolite Calendars

Tick, tick, plop. That's the sound of a coprolite clock. Yes, fossil feces can help record the passage of time. How? It has to do with layers of rock.

Geologists use layers of rock and the fossils they contain to divide up the past. Think of the layers of clothes on the floor of your bedroom. The top layer was yesterday, the next layer down, two days ago, and so on. Rock layers work the same way except they "tell time" in thousands of years, not days.

What geologists love to find is an "event layer" — a layer of rock that is the same all around the world. This can happen when a huge meteorite hits the Earth. The ash it shoots into the air falls to Earth and forms a thin event layer over the entire planet. No matter where they are, rocks just above this layer are all the same age, and so are the rocks just below the event layer. Knowing this helps scientists more accurately pinpoint when things happened.

Some rock layers are so chock full of ancient fish coprolites that they become a kind of event layer, too. (These are nicknamed "Crapper events" in honor of the legendary maker of flush toilets, Thomas Crapper.) Like other event layers, the Crapper events help scientists synchronize their rock clocks.

Lesson #2: Ancient Medicine Coprolites

Got the runs? Try a tea made from the leaves of old man's head with a dash of cashew bark and leaves. Sound nasty? Well, if you were a kid in northern Brazil during the Stone Age and had life-threatening diarrhea, you'd be gulping it down. How do we know? Because coprolites pack a double whammy when it comes to understanding ancient diseases and medicines. Sometimes they contain both the culprit and the cure.

Archaeologists have found loads of 7000- to 8000-year-old human turds in a rock shelter called Boqueirão da Pedra Furada in northern Brazil. When paleoparasitologists (scientists who study ancient parasites) did a poop check, they found eggs from whipworms and hookworms.

These nasty microscopic intestinal parasites cause abdominal pain, bloody diarrhea and loss of appetite. Both parasites are still around today.

So how did the ancient Brazilians battle these intestinal invaders? The poop also has the answer. The coprolites contain lots of pollen from cashew and old man's head plants — the same plants used today by indigenous Brazilians to brew a tea for treating intestinal inflammation and diarrhea.

Lesson #3: America's First Beetle Invasion

What did the Pilgrims bring with them on their famous *Mayflower* journey to America in 1620? The official record says the only animals on board were two dogs. But the poop tells a different story. It turns out there were probably lots of six-legged stowaways on board — beetles. How did scientists find out?

In the mid-1990s, archaeologists in Boston, Massachusetts, excavated a privy used not long after the *Mayflower* dropped anchor. An archaeoentomologist (a scientist who studies ancient insects) went snooping through the pile. To her amazement, she found the remains of forty-four species of beetles preserved in the composted poop and household wastes.

But the biggest surprise was

where the insects came from. More than half of the species were European beetles, and almost all were the oldest examples ever found in North America. So while the *Mayflower* passengers thought they were leaving the Old World behind, it turns out they were actually bringing lots of it with them.

Lesson #4: Evolution from the Bottom Up

Evidence of our earliest ancestors is in excrement.

Two billion years ago, all life on Earth was in the oceans. Most of the creatures were made of only a single cell, like bacteria. The big question is: when did the first multi-celled animals, called metazoans, make the scene?

Paleontologists have scoured rocks looking for fossil remains of metazoans, but without much luck. Then, in the early 1980s, Eleanora Robbins, working with the U.S. Geological Survey, had an idea. Perhaps they were looking at the question from the wrong end.

Today microscopic shrimp-like ocean creatures called copepods produce lots of poop, which is hard and accumulates on the ocean floor. But when the copepods die, their bodies quickly decay. *Hmmm,* Eleanora thought. Could the first metazoan poop also have outlasted the pooper?

Eleanora collected really old rocks from around the world and looked for copepod-like coprolites. Bingo! Rocks as old as 1.9 billion years were full of tiny metazoan poop, making them the earliest evidence of metazoan life. She'd proved that in the search for the evolution of life, it's often better to start at the bottom.

Lesson #5: The Poop on Flower Power

It's one of nature's greatest dances: insects eat a flower's pollen and nectar and then, without knowing it, carry some of that pollen to fertilize neighboring flowers. But when did insects and flowering plants start to do this amazing pollen polka? The answer is in the feces.

Scientists trying to tell the insect–flower story usually compare the shape of ancient flowers with that of insects' mouthparts and look for lock-and-key fits. But one group of scientists got really lucky. Looking through their microscope at ancient fossil flowers from Georgia, U.S.A., they noticed tiny spiral and oblong blobs. *Dung-gone-it,* they thought. They kind of look like tiny turds.

A closer look with a powerful scanning electron microscope confirmed it. Yep, those blobs were coprolites all right. They even contained the remains of chewed bits of pollen.

When the scientists compared these fossil feces with fresh stuff from living beetles (known to eat flower pollen and

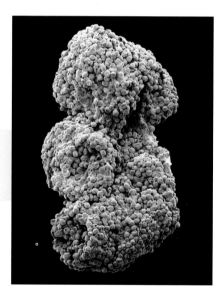

Microscopic ancient beetle poop that's full of pollen grains

pollinate the flowers) the two looked like long-lost turd twins. The tiny coprolites proved that beetles and flowers have been doing the pollen polka for at least 84 million years!

Hendrik Poinar

Scientists love DNA (the stuff from which genes are made) because, like a fingerprint, it tells a lot about the owner. They can extract ancient DNA from fossil bones and teeth. What about from coprolites?

If you want to get DNA from a coprolite, Hendrik Poinar's the man to see. In his lab at McMaster University in Hamilton, Ontario, he's the king for teasing DNA from ancient feces. And that's no easy feat.

When Hendrik was in university his professors said, "No way, we've tried. Dung can't be undung." But Hendrik wouldn't give up. After all, he was the son of George Poinar, the ancient insect expert whose work inspired the book *Jurassic Park,* in which scientists get dino DNA from a fossil mosquito. If Dad had Jurassic Park, then Junior wanted Jurassic Poop.

Hendrik had some well-preserved 20 000-year-old coprolites from Gypsum Cave, near Las Vegas, Nevada. He was sure there was DNA in that dung, but how to get it out?

Hendrik had read a news story about a new drug for diabetics. The drug, called PTB, removes the crusty buildup of sugars from the walls of diabetics' blood vessels. *Wow,* thought Hendrik. Maybe the sugars in old poop stick together like those in a diabetic. Could these sticky sugars have trapped the DNA? It was worth a try. Hendrik mixed a sample of his Gypsum Cave coprolite with PTB and *presto* — there was the DNA of an extinct giant ground sloth.

Hendrik believes that ancient DNA has endless lessons to teach. This genetic information may help tell us why and how the giant Ice Age animals went extinct, if Neanderthals were able to speak (talking is linked to certain genes), and even whether Stone Age boys and girls had different diets (with DNA you can tell if the pooper was male or female). All this genetic gold from the humblest of fossils.

Message to the Future

Suppose one of your poops became a coprolite. It would send a special message about you to future scientists. Think about five things you want the scientists to be able to learn from your 21st-century coprolite. Here's an example:

The Evidence	The Message
Lots of wildflower pollen	That kid loved honey.
A piece of chicken bone	Definitely not a vegetarian.
A dog hair	Probably didn't eat Rover, just had a pet.
Watermelon seeds	Must be a summer poop.
No parasites	Had clean water and food.

Lesson #6: Bunny Tonight

How did ancient Americans eat? If you were a kid growing up in the American southwest 7000 years ago, your parents weren't bugging you to chew your food. *Don't fool with your food, son. Swallow it whole!*

Ancient coprolites found in caves from Colorado to Mexico show that chewing was definitely bad cave manners. One dried human doo-doo found in a cave in Mexico's Tehuacan Valley contained the whole skeleton of a harvest mouse. Coprolites from Hinds Cave in Texas contain everything from raccoon claws to a bird foot — with all the bones still attached.

The coprolites also revealed that ancient American moms and dads didn't spend a lot of time

sweating over a cooking fire. Of the hundreds of bones found in the human coprolites in these caves, only a few are charred. A more typical recipe? Take one cottontail rabbit. Crush to break bones. Tear apart. Eat.

The downside of all this furry fast food? There's evidence that many kids died from choking and adults from blocked intestines. Hmmm ... maybe there *is* something to chewing before you swallow.

The Future of Fossil Feces

What does the future hold for fossil feces? Scientists around the world are now searching coprolites for DNA, parasites, food remains and pollen in an effort to understand the past.

And as more scientists start "listening" to coprolites, there are more and more surprise discoveries. Like this one: you're looking at a picture of the inside of a spiral fish coprolite that's more than 40 million years old. It's been sliced in half, like cutting a loaf of bread in two.

This fossilized fish feces is from Mali, Africa, which from 40 to 70 million years ago was covered by a large, shallow sea. A tiny clam drilled into this rocky rectal remnant creating a tear-shaped hole. Why, you ask? Because the clam was making itself a home. It's the first coprolite clam cavern ever found. Proof that the final lesson from leavings is one we can all take to heart: Whether it's a mansion or a mound, there's no poop like home.

An ancient fish coprolite with a hole drilled by a clam

Glossary

archaeologists — scientists who learn about past humans by studying their remains, including graves, buildings, tools and pottery

carnivores — animals such as dogs, seals and cats whose main food is other animals

cololites — digested food found fossilized in an ancient animal's intestines

coprolites — fossil feces, either frozen, dried or turned to stone

feces — what's left of food when it has passed through an animal's body

fossils — the remains of ancient animals or plants, usually preserved through drying or turning into rock

trace fossils — fossils of things produced by an ancient animal or plant, including eggs, coprolites, footprints and leaf impressions

herbivores — animals that eat plants

lithifying — the gradual process of a dead animal or plant turning into stone

paleontologists — scientists who study fossil remains of ancient plants and animals, including dinosaurs

parasites — creatures that live in or on another plant or animal and get their food by eating their host

phosphates — chemicals that are a main nutrient for plants and an important part of animal bones

pollen — dustlike grains produced by the male part of a plant to fertilize the female egg

tyrannosaurids — a group of two-legged, meat-eating dinosaurs that includes *Tyrannosaurus rex* and *Daspletosaurus torosus*

Answers

You Be the Poop Detective, page 11: The real coprolite is on the left. Found in Florida, it's probably an alligator coprolite. Compare it with the crocodile coprolite on page 8. The imposter coprolite was made using the recipe on page 20.

Solve the Case of Who Dung It, page 25: It's from a mosasaur. Ancient marine reptile coprolites like this one are commonly found in this area of Texas.

Are You an Outhouse Detective?, page 33: (1) apple seeds, (2) corn, (3) a peach pit, (4) cherry pits, (5) a marble (which suggests that at least one outhouse user was a child).

Photo Credits

Page 6: SEPM (Society for Sedimentary Geology). **Page 8:** (left) Hendrik Poinar, McMaster University; (middle) Peter Frank, reproduced with permission from the Canadian Museum of Nature, Ottawa, Canada; (right) Paul Davidson; (in magnifier) © 2005 Canadian Museum of Nature, Ottawa, Canada, photo by Steve Cumbaa. **Page 9:** Paul Davidson. **Page 10:** (top) Peter Frank, © 2005. Reproduced with permission from the Canadian Museum of Nature, Ottawa, Canada; (right) Karl Reinhard; (bottom) Peter Frank, reproduced with permission from the Canadian Museum of Nature, Ottawa, Canada. **Page 11:** (left and right) Paul Davidson. **Page 14:** © Stephen J. Krasemann/DRK PHOTO. **Page 16:** Hendrik Poinar, McMaster University. **Page 17:** Wendy Sloboda. **Page 19:** Coprolite from the collection of the Canadian Museum of Nature, Ottawa, Canada © Jake Berkowitz. **Page 20:** Paul Davidson. **Page 23:** Paul Davidson. **Page 24:** Hendrik Poinar, McMaster University. **Page 25:** Paul Davidson. **Page 27:** HARRISFROMPARIS.COM. **Page 28:** Hendrik Poinar, McMaster University. **Page 29:** Glenna W. Dean. **Page 33:** Vaughn M. Bryant. **Page 36:** © The Field Museum, #PP44627. **Page 37:** Chantall Van Raay. **Page 38:** Photo provided by Leif Tapanila, under the support of the L.S.B. Leakey Foundation awarded to Maureen A. O'Leary.

Index